Who Stole Your
Identity?

DARE TO BE THE PERSON
YOU ALWAYS WANTED TO BE

*Dear Desiree:
Hope you enjoy my book -
It was a pleasure meeting you

Sincerely,
Tooth Bosd*

Who Stole Your
Identity?

DARE TO BE THE PERSON
YOU ALWAYS WANTED TO BE

DR. ISORA BOSCH

WESTBOW®
PRESS
A DIVISION OF THOMAS NELSON
& ZONDERVAN

WestBow Press books may be ordered through booksellers or by contacting:

WestBow Press
A Division of Thomas Nelson & Zondervan
1663 Liberty Drive
Bloomington, IN 47403
www.westbowpress.com
1 (866) 928-1240

Because of the dynamic nature of the Internet, any web addresses or links contained in this book may have changed since publication and may no longer be valid. The views expressed in this work are solely those of the author and do not necessarily reflect the views of the publisher, and the publisher hereby disclaims any responsibility for them.

Any people depicted in stock imagery provided by Thinkstock are models, and such images are being used for illustrative purposes only. Certain stock imagery © Thinkstock.

ISBN: 978-1-4908-7676-4 (sc)
ISBN: 978-1-4908-7677-1 (e)

Library of Congress Control Number: 2015905995

Print information available on the last page.

WestBow Press rev. date: 04/28/2015

Contents

Dedication

I want to dedicate this book to my parents, who taught me the value of education and gave me unconditional love and support.

Foreword

As the coordinator of psychology classes at an inner-city community college, I was always on the lookout for excellent teachers of psychology. To connect with our students and to stimulate their interest in this subject, which is so relevant to the lives we lead, teachers must be able to make connections to the people sitting before them, must be able to see beyond their surface enthusiasm or malaise—or fear or anger—to the truth of the person that lies within. The day that Dr. Isora Bosch walked into my office, a woman with extraordinary experiences ranging from holding senior management positions with the city government of New York to leading numerous workshops on topics such as anger management and posttraumatic stress, I was confident that I had hit the jackpot. And how right I was.

Over the next ten years, I had the pleasure of working closely with Dr. Bosch. Her energy and enthusiasm were impressive, but what was really unusual about her approach to her students was her willingness to see the real "them." Inside the classroom her students, many of whom were used to working in isolation to achieve a grade, learned to work in groups supporting each other's efforts. And she herself was willing to go outside the classroom to offer assistance when it was needed and in whatever form it was needed. That sometimes meant buying lunch, making connections to outside agencies, offering advice, providing emotional support and encouragement. She had a powerful impact on the lives of many of her students, and the connections she forged with them have lasted over the years.

I came to know Dr. Bosch, too, as a powerful speaker and translator of psychological theory into useful life lessons. She is clearly a person who is at ease in her own skin and who exudes confidence and control. In life-coaching classes, she has attracted a wide variety of people, some of whom are looking for a way to find within themselves these qualities that she so clearly possesses, some who are unhappy with themselves or with some aspect of their life situations. In these classes, she is able to use her skills as a facilitator to encourage individual reflection and sensitive group discussion of habits and behaviors that are shaped by participants' earliest relationships and that come to define them while actually remaining outside their conscious awareness. Using concepts of giants in the fields of behavioral health, she is able to give participants in her workshops a structure to better understand both the process by which they have come to their present position in life and the means to step back, reassess, and change that position to one of their own choosing.

Now, in writing *Who Stole Your Identity?*, Dr. Bosch has provided this same opportunity to the reader. What a tremendous service to the curious and the searching who want to better understand themselves; to the discontented who want to understand the source of their unhappiness; to the wounded who want to heal. Beginning with the idea of "traditional teaching habits," she explains how our earliest learning experiences are often the root of later problems. By simply taking in the assumptions and the values that we are fed by others, without reflection and without personal understanding and commitment, we have been set up for a life lived in the shadow of others. The irrational thinking, poor self-esteem, and emotional suffering that are so commonly found in our world today are the result.

Through a thoughtful introduction to psychological concepts, followed by questions for reflection and exercises designed to encourage the process of reflection, Dr. Bosch has provided a means of revisiting those earliest experiences and reconsidering the lessons learned. Most important, she has created the opportunity for readers to redefine themselves, becoming the people they have the potential to be.

In *Who Stole Your Identity?*, Dr. Bosch has provided an invaluable compass for all who are looking to change course or to more fully understand the direction their lives have taken. I can think of no one better to act as mentor and guide on such a challenging journey.

Joan Rafter, PhD

Preface

My motivation to write this book developed progressively. My interest grew due to several events in my life. In the 1980s, when I started working on my doctoral degree in adult education, I became fascinated with the affective dimension of learning. I developed a special interest in learning more about how identifying and understanding our deepest feelings can positively influence our behavior. We learn to be comfortable with ourselves even if others do not agree with us.

Working with adults, I realize how painful this learning experience can be because it calls for a reevaluation of who we are and of the standards we have been living by for a long time. During those days that I was doing group work with Latinas, I observed how some gender stereotypes shaped their beliefs, attitudes, and behaviors. This observation lent support to the importance of reflection as a valuable tool to understand the way in which we often internalize what we learn through patterns of fear and/or repression.

Over time, I started stressing to my clients how in order to find the true self that is hidden inside them, first they must make major changes or modifications in the way they think and act. It is my opinion that adults, instead of believing that everything they do is correct because others said it is so, should ask, Why must I do it? Is this what I really want? Even though I have worked mainly with women, a significant number of male clients have also identified behaviors, influenced by past experiences, that hindered their personal growth.

I always had an interest in the concept of identity. In 2004, I was interviewed for a special report on Latinas' health that was going to be published in a well-known magazine. It was then that I realized how significant this subject is. My comments were published under the topic, "Make Time to Search inside Your Soul." According to the magazine, in our twenties, some of us graduated from college and left our parents' home; we then asked ourselves, And now what? I said that it was normal to feel confusion during this period when our identities began taking shape. On one hand, we want to please our parents; on the other hand, we start developing our own ideas about what we want. It was my opinion that because of this contradiction, it was not easy to struggle with the conflicting loyalties. This could be especially difficult for Latinas because of the strong influence of their cultural values in their development.

In 2002, I gave an interview to a Hispanic newspaper about Latinos in this country. I pointed out that we need to be open to new ways of thinking in order to find our true identity. These comments are reflected in this book. My experience working as an educator, in a variety of roles, taught me that learning new things is very important if we want to live a better life. Our environment, socioeconomic status, and socialization process are significant components in our identity development. However, only through the reflection of our experiences and self-knowledge can we define our internal reality: who we really are, and what makes us different from others.

When I started to teach Psychology of Women, I developed an even better understanding of how sex or gender stereotypes often influence the way in which women decide to live their lives. In the past, based on tradition, men had more power and had to work while women stayed home. The egalitarian position states that both sexes have the same rights and power.

I think that we are not there yet. We are in a stage of transition where many people think that men and women have the same right to devote the same amount of time to work and family life. However, women are generally expected to focus on the family and men on work. One of the consequences of this way of thinking, which is a result of what we learned during our childhood, is women's denial of their real identity. This often happens because they are afraid they could be a threat to conservatives or because they do not want to feel guilty.

Based on what I have learned through many years during my presentations in different countries, this attitude is more common among some ethnic groups, but it is universal. I think that this topic of finding your personal identity often relates to women. However, several men with whom I have discussed my book have told me that they also have not been able to stop being a victim of cultural taboos. They mentioned that this often makes it difficult to show the world who they really are, instead of trying to please others.

In 2008 I wrote an article about my group work with women. This experience increased my motivation and enthusiasm to write this book. One of the most important tasks of participants in my groups was to analyze how culture influenced the way in which they learned to perceive the world and their behavior. Reflecting on their beliefs, their values, and most of all, on others' expectations was of great value. They realized how their desires were not taken into consideration.

Participants' reflections often showed that they feel guilty when their actions are not in agreement with the cultural patterns that dictate their behavior; they are afraid to upset others or to face their rejection. Guilt is often defined by the participants as "feeling in pain when you do something that goes against what others expect." One of the consequences this may have is self-generated stress.

Based on my observations, regardless of whether these women were intelligent or successful in several aspects of their lives, becoming the person they wanted to be was not always possible. The small group experience offered participants the support and structure that they needed to explore their lives, engage in a search for their real selves, and incorporate these new persons into their lives. During the evaluation process, participants often affirmed that the best thing that happened to them was to start making decisions on their own, regardless of what others expected from them or what they might say.

The goal of my groups, and of this book, is to motivate those individuals who are interested in redesigning their lives, and also to motivate those who feel they are not ready yet to think about themselves and to love themselves more by becoming the people they really want to be. These are essential ingredients to live a more satisfying life, to better cope with stressful situations, and to bring life into balance.

I am sure that many of the concepts I use in this book will help readers label those feelings that they have been having for a long time, but often have not been able to express. This is very important when we try to break free of some things from the past that we know are hurting us, and when we want to incorporate new learning into our system of beliefs, values, and behavior. I have no doubt that this book will be the beginning of a long trip that offers plenty of options. It will offer the freedom you need to use new experiences to continue growing and improving each day. Knowledge gives us the freedom we need so that we can stop being passive observers of our lives, and so that we can play a more active role in the direction we want our lives to take.

I want to express my gratitude to my clients for sharing their lives with me and trusting me to guide them. They have been my inspiration and motivation to continue to learn and to ask questions. This book is a reflection of the self-transformation of so many people who allowed me to enter into and touch their lives.

This journey would not have been possible without the love and support of so many people, scattered around the world, who encouraged me to try to know and understand myself. Thanks for being patient, listening to my ideas, offering me suggestions and editing advice, and for your never-ending support. You really confirm that with love and a helping hand from others, everything is possible—even discovering who you really are.

I want to thank Dora Pozzi for reading the first manuscript and giving me valuable feedback. I must acknowledge Dr. Joan Rafter and Martha Becker for their helpful suggestions and constructive comments. Thanks also to Diego Silva, graphic designer, for helping me select the design of the book cover.

Introduction

The purpose of this book is to offer a practical guide to start a process of self-exploration; it provides a framework to analyze your past experiences, search for your true self, and incorporate this new person into your life. What you will learn will help you recover or rediscover your identity, which is crucial in the course of your personal growth. This will result in the increase of self-awareness and self-confidence, the use of strategies to take better care of yourself, and the implementation of changes that will lead to a life full of peace and inner harmony.

Who Stole Your Identity? will be of interest to you if you have ever wondered who you would really like to be. During this journey, you will also learn to more easily identify and manage those things that create unnecessary stress and that perhaps hinder your personal growth. Self-knowledge is one of the most important aspects of this book, since it is my opinion that only by searching your inner self can you discover, accept, and celebrate the person you really are.

This book will help you eliminate those barriers that prevent you from living how you would really like to, in harmony with those values that you consider important in life. Once you achieve your true identity, coping with life stressors will be easier. You will realize that you frequently generate your own stress, and you will understand how your thoughts can often control your life. Sometimes we perceive life challenges as worse than they really are; this happens because in the past, we have learned to think and behave in a certain way.

The first chapter will help you understand how many times, without realizing it, you live based on what you have learned early in life. As a result, sometimes you behave unconsciously and automatically, although later on you may feel that behavior is not the one that really satisfies you. As a consequence, there are times in which you let others define your identity and steal your opportunity of finding out what makes you unique and different from others. *Identity* is defined as "the set of beliefs and values that determine the way a person thinks and behaves." In the attempt to discover your identity, you are influenced by your family and significant others in your life, your culture, the society you live in, the profession or occupation you chose, and by many other factors that shape your vision of the world.

Finding your identity—discovering the person you really want to be—requires an internal dialogue and time for reflection. You will also need the courage to make changes or modifications in certain perceptions, attitudes, and behavior. Having the ability for self-reflection and understanding the motives for your behavior form the cornerstone for finding out your true identity. This is the way you start developing more self-confidence and self-love—essential ingredients in the personal growth process of any human being.

The exercises in this book will help you better manage life challenges and behave according to your own standards and values. You will learn to use self-care activities to improve the quality of your life and replenish your energy. You will have the opportunity to analyze the link between your beliefs, thoughts, and behaviors by identifying ways of thinking that might negatively affect your emotional well-being. Socrates, the Greek philosopher, stated, "The unexamined life is not worth living."[1]

Of special interest will be to understand the importance of reflecting and writing about what you think and to complete autobiographic exercises that might lead to a deeper perception of your life. These exercises might also help you identify your strengths. It is possible that you may discover wonderful aspects about yourself that you had never thought about. I invite you to embark in this personal growth journey to redesign your life and stop living according to others' desires and assumptions. At the end, you will enjoy a sense of freedom because as Epictetus, the Greek philosopher, said, "Is freedom anything else than the right to live as we wish? Nothing else."[2]

CHAPTER 1

I Have the Right to Be Who
I Really Want to Be

It is time to see yourself as the person you want to be.

If our most important concern in life is what others might think about us, then we are living according to someone else's rules, which might prevent us from discovering our potential and our passion in life. Based on my experience as a life coach and therapist, understanding the idea of "traditional teaching habits" has been very helpful in working with my clients. It helps them to understand why they often live based on others' standards and how their lives might be controlled by what they learned in the past.

This teaching style conveys knowledge without initiating a dialogue. It makes most people accept certain concepts—especially about what is right or wrong—that are repeated later in life without any reasoning or challenge. The problem is that when they make the transition into adult life, they may realize that to behave according to those learned concepts might be convenient to others but destructive to them.

This quote by Plutarch, the Greek philosopher, helps us to understand this concept: "The mind is not a vessel to be filled but a fire to be kindled."[1] What one of the participants in one of my personal development groups said after learning about traditional teaching habits, clearly explains why this concept is so helpful in finding out who we really are: "It helped us put a label to what we were feeling. ... It was like breaking the chains." In order to have a sense of freedom, sometimes we need to question and challenge some of the values and beliefs transmitted by family, religion, culture, and society. Becoming passive recipients of opinions and attitudes based on traditional values might interfere with our emotional well-being; it may make us use strategies to handle life challenges that are very far from being healthy.

We can only make positive changes in our lives if we are able to connect the past and the present. We all have a child of the past living inside us. The way we handle problems is related to our childhood and the behaviors we learned to face difficult situations. Our words and actions are determined by the set of beliefs, worldviews, and opinions that we have developed during our lifetime. Beliefs are formed from facts and assumptions. Those based on assumptions—often buried deep in our minds—later become irrational generalizations.

When we are trying to change, we bring that prior knowledge into the learning situation; it forms the basis for the construction of new knowledge. Changing does not mean totally rejecting what we had believed for a long time, but giving meaning to and reconciling old learning (the habits we learned through traditional teaching) with what we are currently learning. This generally leads us to expand our perspectives about life, to see things in a new light.

In order for human beings to live the lives they want, they must challenge those values and beliefs they have learned through tradition. As adults, we need to determine whether we are satisfied with the people we have become. Sometimes not being satisfied with who we are makes us experience a sense of poor self-esteem and self-confidence. We must create our own reality instead of continuing to do what we think is correct or what we have always been doing because it is what traditional values call for. If our behavior is based on the expectations of others, it means that we are not considering the options we have in life; it is those other people who are in control.

It is important to understand that changing does not mean forgetting the beliefs and values we already have. Instead, in order to be true to ourselves, we must decide what to keep and what we should get rid of. I have observed that group participants often have some of those experiences that may change people's lives when they suddenly become aware of something that they had never suspected. This is known as a "click experience." It takes place when people make connections between the traditional knowledge acquired in the past and those behaviors that are currently limiting their personal growth. This happens when during a coaching session a client suddenly realizes that in order to please others, she is not being true to herself. This habit has been so deeply embedded in her brain that the behavior was never questioned.

The most important discovery, then, is becoming aware that others are deciding what we want without giving us the opportunity to express our opinions. In other words, our behaviors are not based on true feelings; we have been living most of our adult lives giving others control of our emotions. When we use this concept of traditional teaching habits to analyze our lives, we finally realize that others cannot control our lives unless we give them permission to do so. The way we respond to others' desires is our option. We must realize that the decision about how we act is ours to make, regardless of what others taught us to believe.

Self-Generated Stress

We create most of our stress, which is very dangerous since when we generate this type of stress it is difficult to be aware of what we are doing. Self-generated stress originates in our perception, and it is often unconscious. When we live based on other people's standards, we are often doing things that are not making us very happy, and as a consequence, we create our own stress. The first thing that we need to do to manage self-generated stress is to develop awareness of those events or people who make us lose sight of who we really are and of what we want. It is important to be aware of our reactions and of the messages that we send ourselves.

Finally, we need to understand that something about the way we think and behave needs to be modified, that we must pay attention to what is going on in our bodies and minds, and that we must be more responsible for our physical, emotional, and spiritual well-being. Stress is only negative when we believe that we lack the capacity to cope with life challenges. The way we interpret and manage these challenges will determine if we are going to feel that we are in control over our lives and if we will learn to successfully cope with problems in the future.

It is essential that we learn to identify what "pushes our buttons." Learn to listen to your body. Do you feel that your muscles begin to tense when you have to talk to that person who always puts you in a bad mood? Does the idea of visiting that relative you really do not like make you crazy? These are signs of stress. Be aware of what is happening and when it happens. What messages are you sending yourself in these situations?

In order to start a new relationship with ourselves and to avoid situations that may increase our stress level, we must get rid of our false expectations. We often keep waiting for significant people in our lives to change or we wait for a miracle to take place. We usually generate our own stress by having false expectations of ourselves and of others. When we finally learn that there are things that we will never be able to change, we will realize that we are the ones who need to change. A perfect example is when women are in unhealthy relationships but expect that with time and like magic, their partners will change their behavior.

A human being is not like a car that you take to a mechanic to have it fixed. People must have the desire and motivation to change. This will not happen because you want it to happen. When our expectations are realistic, we are able to manage our lives with more ease. Sometimes it is preferable not to expect that much from those people who, we know deep in our hearts, cannot give us what we desire.

Learning to manage stress in order to rediscover ourselves goes beyond obtaining information we were not aware of earlier; it implies a critical review of our assumptions, our perceptions, and our willingness to develop new ways of thinking. After all, more important than the actual events that cause our stress, is our perception of them. Remember that problems are opportunities to learn. It is our responsibility to accept challenge and to identify new ways of thinking and behaving. Do you want to become a victim of situations that cause stress in life, or do you want to face challenges with determination, confidence, and hope?

Transforming Irrational Self-Talk

If you want to set realistic goals, first you must create your own vision of life. Take time to think what makes you happy, what gives you joy and satisfaction. Sometimes the voices inside us make our lives more difficult. We practice irrational self-talk, think about things that took place a long time ago, and allow negative experiences of the past to influence our present. Here are some examples of irrational self-talk:

- There is nothing I can do to change and improve my present situation.
- I do not deserve the good things that others have.
- I failed as a parent.
- I will never know what I really want.
- If I say that I don't know, others will think I am incompetent.
- I have no control over my emotions.
- If I offer my opinion, I might look stupid.
- If I was not able to change before, I know for sure that I will not be able to change now.

The good news is that since we create these irrational thoughts, we can also eliminate them. Once we identify them, we can learn to counter or reframe them in a more rational fashion. When we start practicing rational self-talk, we start believing in what we are saying. In the following chapter, we will discuss how to change the way we think so that we can become more rational and optimistic persons.

In order for this transformation to take place, we need to learn to reflect in solitude. This is the kind of reflection that helps us analyze what we have learned. During this process, we try to reach out to those aspects of ourselves that have been confused or insecure until we are finally able to discover our emotional selves. Reflecting in solitude requires taking our mind to places where we sometimes refuse to go because of the pain this might cause. In other words, we do not learn because of what happens to us, but rather, when we do something about it and when we analyze what has happened. Life experiences are valuable lessons when we reflect on them, learn from them, and apply the new learning in our daily lives.

* * * * * *

Exercise 1: Questions for Reflection

- Are you happy with who you are? Do you live according to your values and standards? Most of the time do you live to make others happy, forgetting what you really want?

- Identify the major sources of stress in your life. What makes you feel anxious? What pushes your buttons or makes you lose control? How does this relate to what you learned early in life?

- Identify those things that cause your stress. Which of those do you think you can change, and which do you think you cannot change? What would you like to do about them?

- What is your passion in life? Is this passion your driving force in life?

- Have you decided what makes you happy, or did you let others define it for you? Explain.

Exercise 2: Self-Reflection

I need to focus on the following in order to improve the quality of my life:

- managing stress
- managing anger
- decision-making
- communication/expressing my feelings
- scheduling time for myself
- work/career
- balancing personal and work life
- interpersonal relationships
- personal development
- home/family
- social life
- spirituality
- health/nutrition/fitness
- finances
- other

Comments:

CHAPTER 2

Rethinking the Way You Think

There is nothing either good or bad but thinking makes it so.[1]
—William Shakespeare, English dramatist

Our thoughts can cause episodes of distress; even those thoughts that at a given time seem normal and rational to us can sometimes become our worst enemies. Your mind can determine your feelings and actions. According to Dr. Aaron T. Beck's cognitive behavior therapy (CBT),[2] this is a product of our beliefs, which often control what we think we must do with our lives. Those "have to" and "must do" beliefs often create inner conflict. It would be good to ask ourselves, "Am I doing what my heart is really asking me to do?" or "Am I doing what I think I must do to please others, although I know this is not what I want?"

Albert Ellis was an American psychologist who developed a theory to explain the relationship between events/situations and emotions. This is known as the rational emotive behavior therapy (REBT).[3] According to his theory, our beliefs can create emotional suffering. However, this suffering is not a response to events or situations, but to the thoughts or beliefs we have about what is happening to us. In other words, what we think influences our emotions and actions. According to this theory, we are more concerned about being loved or accepted by others than by loving ourselves. One of his quotes reflects this thought: "I get people to truly accept themselves unconditionally, whether or not their therapist or anyone loves them."[4]

When you make an effort to see problems in a different way, you may become aware of the irrational beliefs and assumptions that you often have about yourself. This manifests in thoughts that are generally unconscious and automatic; they are not determined by logic or reflection. If you make a list of these thoughts, you will understand how they limit your behavior. The good news is that once you start acknowledging this, you can create new thoughts. These thoughts replace and help to eliminate the irrational ones. This helps you to behave in a more rational fashion.

These are examples of irrational thoughts we are often victims of:

- I am not supposed to say no.
- I must be perfect.
- I must be liked and accepted by everyone.
- I should do whatever it takes not to disappoint others.
- I should not think about myself.
- I am afraid to be alone.
- I should not let others know how I feel.
- If I do not have others' approval, I am worthless.
- I know that my past determines my present.
- I am responsible for the problems of my family.
- I have had these irrational thoughts for so long that I will never be able to change.
- If I end this relationship, people are going to start talking about me.
- If I leave this job, I know that I will not be able to get another one.
- I am so stupid; I am always making mistakes.
- I have no control over my life; everything has already been decided.
- Happiness is a matter of luck.

How Can I Change My Irrational Thoughts?

First you must reflect on the following: When I have to make a decision, do I think about what others feel or could say about me, or do I think about what would make me feel better?

Go back in time and think about your "traditional teaching habits." Are there habits that are of no benefit to you as an adult? Be honest with yourself; do not be afraid to admit the truth. We must accept that during some phase of our lives, we have fallen victim to traditional education; therefore, we need to identify the aspects of that education that could be detrimental to our emotions and eliminate or modify them.

As a coach and therapist, I know that sometimes we prefer the status quo, a Latin expression that means "the current moment or to leave things the way they are." Have you asked yourself why you don't change some aspects of your life with which you are dissatisfied, even though you know you need to change them? Is it possible that you are afraid of the uncertain? What would learning new behaviors bring to your life? Will those persons whom you consider important in your life still love you?

Once you have identified your irrational thoughts and realize how some of the limitations related to your behavior and personal growth are self-imposed, you will create new thoughts to replace them. A more realistic outlook will make you feel better and will give you a burst of energy to better manage stress. Let these new thoughts become your behavior from now on. Here are some examples:

Irrational thought: There is nothing I can do about it.
New thought: Yes, there are always options.

Irrational thought: Sometimes I am afraid to express what I want.
New thought: I have the right to express my true feelings.

Irrational thought: I will never be able to change the way I think.
New thought: I am sure that I can learn new things.

Irrational thought: I will never be able to face this problem.
New thought: I am able to face life's challenges.

Suggestions for Rational Thinking

- Give yourself the opportunity to learn new things.
- Always examine the actual evidence for your assumption.
- When you make a decision, think whether you are being realistic.
- Think what you would tell a friend who always has irrational thoughts.
- Do not blame yourself. Think that you are allowed to make mistakes.
- Do not try to control external circumstances; instead, learn to manage your inner emotions.
- Eliminate "I cannot," and replace it with, "Yes, I can."
- Write empowering statements.
- Be a good friend to yourself. Practice self-compassion; show kindness and understanding toward yourself.
- Think about your own definition of success and happiness. Do not let others define those for you.
- Develop goals and put them into practice; think in advance what you will do when you find obstacles that could prevent you from achieving your goals.
- Understand that your current way of thinking might not be the best one; perhaps it is having a negative effect on your emotional well-being.
- Be flexible; reevaluate your goals regularly and make the appropriate changes.
- Establish an emotional support system. Seek the support of people who are really important in your life. Try to stay away from negative people.
- Do not be afraid of changing because others might reject you when you become the person you want to be. Perhaps the consequences will be better than you think.

* * * * * *

Exercise 1

Write down the irrational thoughts that are most harmful in your life and under them write down the new thoughts that will replace them from now on.

Exercise 2: Now Respond to the Following Questions

- What is the worst that could happen if you change the way you think at present?

- What do you fear the most?

- What would be the consequences of your new behavior?

- What is the best thing that could happen to you if you change the way you currently think? How would this change your life?

- What can you do to cope with your fears of changing?

Perhaps after responding to these questions, you will become aware of the fact that the consequences are not as awful as you thought. Furthermore, it might be the best thing that could happen in your life.

CHAPTER 3

Anger Cannot Be Avoided,
but Violence Can Be

Holding on to anger is like grasping a hot coal with the
intent of throwing it at someone else; you are the one who
gets burned.[1]
—Buddha, religious leader

Whether we want to admit it or not, we have been or are still angry at
someone or something. Anger is not a negative feeling; it can give us the
energy we need to make changes in our lives. However, we must learn
how to manage it.

The irrational thoughts that we discussed in chapter 2 often precipitate
our anger. Anger can hinder the attainment of self-knowledge. We must
identify the real problem behind our anger. Are we reacting to what others
expect from us? Are we frustrated because we cannot do things the way we
want to? Do we feel like a victim? Could the problem be that our needs
are not being met?

Anger is often caused by frustration when we do not get what we expect
or want from life or from other people. Sometimes others cannot offer us
what we expect from them. Other times we are unable to accept a situation
that is not under our control. All we can do in both cases is to become fully
aware of how we are the ones who must change.

Not being able to regulate our emotions, including anger, is one of the main sources of stress. First we must define the real reason for our anger, what are the underlying feelings or thoughts? Is it caused by fear, frustration, or insecurity? We also have to take into consideration that when anger is suppressed or it is not expressed appropriately it may lead to medical problems. Our bodies' physical responses to uncontrolled anger include a pounding heart, cold hands, headache, stomachache, and dry mouth. These reactions intensify our feelings, making the situation even worse.

I want to emphasize that anger in itself is neither good nor bad; the real challenge is how we express that anger. The following are some of the unhealthy and ineffective ways to manage anger:

- Blowing up and losing control.
- Withdrawing; giving people the silent treatment.
- Avoiding the person or situation that is making us angry.
- Becoming passive-aggressive. We may look like we are going along with the situation and are not angry, when in reality, we are "burning" inside.
- Internalizing the anger. When we "swallow" our anger, we can trigger a wide range of physical problems. Depression can be occasionally caused by turning anger inward.
- Projecting our anger onto others. There are times when we try to deny our anger and instead see others as being angry at us.

Anger does not go away simply because you ignore it, deny it, or are not able to resolve it. It remains there, harming your physical and/or emotional health and your relationships. In order to manage anger appropriately, first you must identify the individuals or situations that make you angry. It is important to reflect on what you are feeling and label the emotions associated with your anger. In addition, you must listen to your body. How does it respond to anger? The more self-knowledge you have and the better you know your body, the more likely that anger will not take you by surprise.

* * * * * *

Exercise 1: Respond to the Following Questions about Anger

It is important that you recognize what triggers your anger. Prior to trying to manage your anger, you must understand why you are angry and who or what you are angry at.

* What makes you angry? Think about a recent situation when you felt angry.

* Who or what were you angry at?

* How did you react? What else were you feeling besides anger? Were there any thoughts or beliefs in particular that were making you angry?

* * * * *

Emotional Intelligence

Emotional intelligence is the ability to perceive, understand, and manage emotions. In 1995, the American psychologist Daniel Goleman made popular the term *emotional intelligence*[2] to describe how emotions often take control of the rational part of the brain and guide our behaviors, especially in situations that are perceived as dangerous or threatening. This makes us react impulsively. According to Goleman, in this case we are being "hijacked" by anger. We must prevent this from happening because when it does, we become irrational and give other people or situations control over our emotions.

Emotionally intelligent people are able to manage their emotions without becoming victims of such a hijack. This concept offers a different perspective and can become a valuable tool for deeper self-knowledge and better management of relationships. Since emotional intelligence facilitates the process of self-awareness, it helps us to better understand our emotions and how they affect those around us. Becoming familiar with the concept of emotional intelligence and putting it into practice can help us manage our anger effectively and with less stress. In order to develop emotional intelligence, we need the following:

- *self-awareness*: being able to get in touch with our emotions
- *self regulation of emotions*: being able to handle conflicts in a healthy and productive fashion, without negative effects
- *empathy*: to interpret and understand others' emotions; being able to put ourselves in others' shoes and to understand emotions through verbal and physical language

When we become emotionally intelligent, we communicate in an assertive and direct style. We realize that we do not have to be aggressive or feel guilty or afraid to express how we really feel. We develop the ability to identify life challenges, not as difficult, but as important events in our lives with the unique meaning of motivating us to learn.

Empathy is extremely important in human coexistence. It helps to better listen to others' points of view without preconceived judgments and to develop tolerance toward those who are different. Empathy leads us to understand that there is no universal truth, but that instead each one of us has our own version of what is true.

It is very difficult to be empathic when we are angry. In those moments we tend to think, "I am right and you are wrong." This negatively affects effective communication with people who have different points of view or perspectives.

* * * * * *

Exercise 2: Self-Awareness

- Try to label your feelings today; reflect on them.

- Do you have feelings from the past that you have never been able to express? What influence do they have in your beliefs and in the person you are now?

Exercise 3: Self-Management of Emotions

Reflect on these questions:

- Do you react or respond to difficult situations? You must understand that when you react, you generally do it with impulsivity, often feeling like a victim. When you respond, you take responsibility for your actions and think about the role you are playing in the situation.

- How do you behave in difficult, unexpected, or uncomfortable situations?

- When responding to stressful situations, are some of your behaviors self-destructive? Are they productive? What is the outcome of your actions?

Exercise 4: Empathy

- Do you try to understand others' point of view? Do you have tolerance for diversity; for people who are different from you?

- Which of these factors prevent you from showing empathy?
  - blaming others
  - refusing to admit your mistakes
  - feeling like a victim
  - making others feel inferior
  - labeling people
  - responding to criticism with criticism

- ○ offering advice before listening because you think that others do not know what they are saying
- ○ always seeing the world through your point of view

- What do you need to do to develop more empathy?

* * * * * *

Forgiving Is Not the Same as Forgetting

Anger often prevents us from forgiving. Forgiving takes a great deal of courage and strength, but most of all, you must do it for your own well-being. During this process, the person who does the forgiving is the one who gets the benefits of it. One of the main benefits is that it helps us see life in a different light, freeing us of destructive feelings such as grief and rage and welcoming a more peaceful present. Experts say that forgiving is the best prescription for emotional and physical well-being.

Being incapable to forgive is one of the main reasons why we often feel so much anger. Holding on to anger and refusing to forgive could be very destructive because you continue to carry the emotional consequences of painful experiences of the past. You have two choices: allowing a painful experience that belongs to your past destroy your present or deciding to start healing through forgiveness.

When you are unable to forgive, you are giving other people or situations control of your emotions; you are giving them permission to run your life. You should not blame others for your misery; you have the power to make your own decisions. We often give external events and other people permission to cause negative emotions, which can cause great damage to our physical, emotional, and spiritual well-being. If we fall victims to the negative experiences of the past or of the mistakes we made, we will never find the way out. It is as if these experiences had stolen our peace and balance in life. When you allow negative events of the past to become a permanent part of your life, you are creating your own suffering. Studies show that when we hold on to our anger and refuse to forgive, we are at high risk for heart disease and other stress-related and emotional disorders such as depression and anxiety.

If you carefully think of the act of forgiving, considering that there are times in life when you must change the way you think, it means that you are determined to positively manage emotions caused by unpleasant past experiences; you refuse to harbor negative feelings of bitterness and resentment. In order to forgive, you must substitute the negative thoughts of people who have offended you with your own positive thoughts and emotions. Instead of continually dwelling on negative experiences, focus on how much you learned from them. Any experience, negative or positive, you go through in life makes you wiser, but only if you reflect on it, learn from it, and try to see it as a life lesson. If you do not reflect on your experiences, they will be meaningless.

* * * * * *

Exercise 5

Forgiving is not an easy process. It means eliminating resentful thoughts from your life. How can you achieve this? Think of a person who hurt you in the past and whom you have not been able to forgive. Ask yourself the following:

- Where does your resentment come from?

- What will be the benefits of forgiving?

- What will be the consequences of continuing to dwell on the same story, of continuing to feel like a victim?

- What is your goal, the desired result of forgiving? Be clear when you formulate your goal. You do not have to feel the need to reconcile, ignore, or forget what the person did to you. If you do this, you will not learn from the experience, and it might happen again.

- What meaning did this experience have in your life? What did you learn from it?

Now enjoy your new feeling. Forgiving will make you feel at peace and will offer you a sense of well-being. Holding on to anger will make you lose a lot of energy that you can use instead in your process of personal development. Finally, do not feel guilty for having taken so long to forgive those who hurt you, for having spent too much energy trying to say goodbye to your anger.

CHAPTER 4

How to Become the Person You Really Want to Be

You can direct the course of your life or allow other people and life circumstances to decide how you live.

Does the word *change* sound too radical to you? I think that most people find it intimidating. Please do not panic. You do not have to make extreme changes; you can start by modifying certain aspects of your life. This seems to be the most difficult transformation stage for my clients. Developing self-awareness is important, accepting that you have to take certain steps to achieve your well-being is great, but now comes the most difficult question: How can I do it? In this chapter I offer some practical suggestions that will hopefully help you in this difficult yet rewarding process that can lead to inner peace.

In this journey to finding your "true self," your thoughts can be your best friends or your worst enemies. Your thoughts follow you; wherever you go, there you find them. They play themselves over and over again in your head. They sometimes say, "I support anything you want to do because I know you will achieve what you want," or they could say, "You will never be able to change or modify your behavior; you will always be the same person you were in the past."

Chapter 2 emphasized the importance of rational thinking in pursuing your goals. If you think rationally, it will be easier to become the person you want to be. A rational and optimistic attitude is the key to finding the motivation to change. If you are convinced that there is nothing you can do to improve your life, you will not take the necessary steps to do it; you will not see the possibility of a better life. You must have self-confidence to be capable of finding your real identity without paying attention to what others might think or say. People with constant irrational thoughts tend to feel inadequate; they often seek the approval of others to do what they want or to pursue their goals.

Rational thinking helps you explore whether your thoughts are based on facts or are the result of past learning, which prescribes how you must think or behave. Being optimistic, but at the same time rational, prompts you to action to transform your life, and when you find obstacles, you think about what you *can* do instead of what you cannot do. I hope that the following suggestions help you find your real identity.

Identify Your Values and Your Passion in Life

You have to begin by opening the drawer where the real you has been hidden, and you must respond to the following question: Who am I when no one is around; when no one is looking at me? Think about what is really important to you. In your opinion, these things are so worthwhile that you want to live according to them. You want people around you to be regardful of them when they interact and communicate with you. Others do not have to agree with your values; however, they must be respectful despite the differences between their own values and yours.

Once you are able to acknowledge your real values, it will be possible for you to develop the rules and principles you want to live by. These values will help you make decisions that you will be satisfied with in all aspects of your life, from long-term goals to daily living. Your values will determine how you choose to respond to any situation you have to face or how you decide to behave with the people around you.

Some examples of things that we value include honesty, loyalty, individuality, ambition, empathy, independence, security, generosity,

27

flexibility, discipline, respect, passion for learning new things, the constant need to face challenges, etc.

Your values could be a combination of your past life experiences within your family; your culture, race, ethnic group, and religious affiliation; and the new things you learn throughout your life. Examples of these are books that you have been reading, formal or informal education, programs you watched on television, a dialogue you had with relatives or friends, counseling or coaching sessions, or any other situation or experience that opened your mind to something you had never thought about before. Make a summary of what you really value in life and analyze whether you have been living according to those values.

Take Responsibility: Do Not Blame Others

You are the architect of your life. Your life will be what you want it to be. You have to stop blaming others because you are not doing what you would like to do or feeling guilty because you want to live according to what you value the most in life. You must understand that people who criticize you when you show your true identity are often behaving in a way that seems very natural and normal to them based on what they learned through traditional teaching habits. If you put yourself in the place of people who have influenced your life, you will understand that they, too, have been victims of this style of education.

You must take responsibility for your life. Refuse to be a victim of others' lives, and decide now that it is your responsibility to determine who you want to be. Let go of your crutches—those excuses on which you have been leaning to avoid facing yourself. It is possible that walking without them might be a little bit difficult at the beginning, but at the end, you will want to run because you will be looking forward to exploring a new world. Every time you start feeling like a victim, shout out loud, "No more excuses; I have the power to change." When you blame others, you deplete yourself of the energy you need to critically reflect on your life.

Put a Stop to Unhealthy Hope

Stop having a false sense of hope: "I do not have time to think about my life now. Once I complete everything I have pending, then I will start." If you keep waiting for the right time to start taking care of and thinking about yourself, you will live a very disappointing life. When you start to think more about yourself, you will have the opportunity to see new perspectives, which in turn will offer you hope and motivation to find out your real identity. Contrary to what many people think, focusing our attention on ourselves does not mean we are selfish; it motivates us to share our reflections with others and perhaps to even facilitate their transformation process.

Be Persistent

Do not focus your attention just on the obstacles you may face or on the negative; think of the positive outcomes that are waiting for you at the end of the road. If you visualize yourself making it to the finish line instead of thinking why you will not be able to accomplish your goals or talking about obstacles all the time, you are being persistent. I agree that it is important to identify the obstacles that you will possibly find, but right away you must try to find the solution to overcome them. To be persistent means confronting anything that might hinder your progress, to continue trying to overcome it with perseverance, and not giving up on the goals you set out to accomplish. As Benjamin Franklin, the American politician said, "Energy and persistence conquer all things."[1]

Take Small Steps

Progress will be your best motivator. Plan to achieve small steps every day, every week, or every month, but make sure that you celebrate each achievement, no matter how small it is, the same way you would celebrate achieving something that you had always desired. You deserve it because you have worked hard to get here; you have the right to be rewarded for work well done. Do not try to accomplish too much within a small period of time because you will be frustrated and might lose motivation.

Be Capable of Forgiving Yourself

One of the main things that you must do to become the person you want to be is to forgive yourself for past mistakes or for not having had the courage to live by your standards. In chapter 3 (Anger Cannot Be Avoided, but Violence Can Be), I discussed the importance of forgiving others. However, we often blame ourselves and feel guilty for our actions. We must make short trips to the past in order to understand our lives, but the only way to live is by moving forward, without looking back too much. This is the only way we can step into a new world of opportunities for learning and growth.

Your traditional teaching habits sometimes make you feel that you must continue doing things the way you are supposed to even when you are not satisfied with your life. You must refuse to be a victim of what happened in the past. Stop feeling sorry about yourself and have the courage to change the way you live. You need to ask yourself the following questions: What will be the outcome of constantly dwelling on my story? Do I want to feel like a victim for the rest of my life?

Talk to Others

Dialogue is one of the best tools we have to make changes in our lives or to modify our behavior. This is why group work is so important, regardless of whether it is a formal or an informal group, or even a group of friends. It is through a dialogue with others that we gain information about our similarities and differences. Sharing our past stories is how we often come to understand how our childhood experiences and our family and social values have shaped who we are. Dialogue offers us new learning; it opens the doors to enriching experiences, which facilitate our transformation. When we allow ourselves to enter other people's worlds and at the same time allow them to enter ours, we expand the possibilities to learn from and with one another, which is rewarding.

Reflect

If you realize that you start to lose focus during your transformation process, reflect on what is happening. Remember, the real meaning of reflection is to process what is going on. Perhaps you need to modify the goals and objectives that you have established in your action plan or you need to think about other options. What really matters is that instead of stopping the process, you take time to reflect and keep moving forward. Reflection takes us to places where we sometimes do not imagine our minds could take us. Sometimes those places are painful, but I want to emphasize that we must go there in order to transform our lives.

Start Writing a Diary

A diary is an excellent tool to facilitate self-reflection, promote personal growth, and help to modify your thoughts and behavior. A diary helps you clarify your personal goals, identify your hopes and fears, discover your strengths, and organize your thoughts. It also helps you document fears and doubts and the progress you have made in the process of personal growth. This is a great exercise to attain "click" experiences, which help us make connections between our behavior, beliefs, values, and thoughts. It is the best way to make sense of our experiences and to make them meaningful.

A diary includes emotions and feelings. It is possible that through it we might discover aspects of our lives that often become part of the intellect, losing the emotional content. As I mentioned earlier, there are emotions that we sometimes keep out of our reach because of the pain they cause. A diary has the power to bring together our rational and affective aspects. When we are writing, no one is listening; we can be honest with ourselves.

Writing a diary can become an ongoing experience that helps you realize that certain behaviors are of benefit to you—or that they may be the enemy. You will start by reflecting on your experiences, on what happens to you, on what you are thinking. Later on, when you read what you have written, you will realize how this information offers the support you need to get more deeply into your reflections. A diary is a great tool for reflecting and obtaining greater insight, which will make it easier to evaluate your progress in the process of personal growth.

What Should I Write, and How Should I Write in My Diary?

Here are a few suggestions:

- Write about a specific topic or simply focus on your feelings, thoughts, concerns, fears, doubts, emotions, expectations, questions about yourself, situations or people in your life, your successes or challenges.
- Use the diary to think about those things in your daily life that give you pleasure or satisfaction and about other aspects that do not make you happy. Remember, the main goal of keeping a diary is to offer you the opportunity to reflect on your experiences.
- When writing about meaningful or significant experiences, think about what happened, why it happened, and what the end result was.
- Be honest and write about whatever comes to mind; do not censure yourself. Just write; do not think whether what you are writing is right or wrong.
- Do not be obsessive about your grammar or spelling. Enjoy the opportunity to be free.
- You do not have to impress anybody; you can write about anything you want or you can draw images that reflect what you are thinking.

* * * * * *

Exercise 1

Make a list of your values and what is most important to you in life.

Exercise 2

Now think: Do you do things with a passion, according to what you value most, or do you simply do them because that is what you think others expect you to do?

Exercise 3

Are you ready to start keeping a diary? Below you will find some ideas that could serve as starting points:

- I can stop adding stress to my life if I learn to ...
- I would be more satisfied with my life if I ...
- This is how I really feel about ...
- I want to tell my friends and/or relatives ...

CHAPTER 5

The Importance of Self-Esteem in Personal Development

No one can make you feel inferior without your consent.[1]
—Eleanor Roosevelt, American First Lady

I define *self-esteem* as the "capacity to love ourselves." In this case, loving ourselves means believing in ourselves and having self-respect, instead of feeling self-doubt and being ashamed of who we are. Sometimes self-love is perceived as selfishness, but I think that in fact it is seeing in ourselves our best friend. How can you love others if you are unable to love yourself?

We have self-esteem when we are capable of having a sense of self-worth and pride. Self-esteem affects your relationship with others: how you choose your partner and your friends, your workplace behavior, how you come across to others, and the determination to live your life the way you want. When you have a healthy level of self-esteem, you embrace and celebrate your strengths. You feel confident about what you do, and when you make a mistake, you see it as a lesson or an opportunity life is offering you to learn something. You are capable of taking risks and not having to feel that you must be perfect. You are optimistic and feel competent to cope with adversity. You learn to find time to take care of yourself. You think about it very carefully before you say yes, and you do not feel guilty when you decide to say no. You are able to express your emotions and to confront those people whose attitudes and behavior sometimes cause you stress.

Low self-esteem may have a negative effect on your emotional well-being. It is one of the main factors that may precipitate depression and anxiety in women as well as in men. However, according to my experience as a therapist, it affects mainly women because of the cultural values they have acquired through traditional teaching habits. Through the socialization process, women often learn to depend on others to feel happy. They also tend to think that they are responsible for others' happiness (especially for their families).

When you have low self-esteem, not only do you feel incompetent at times when coping with a difficult situation, but you also hesitate when you have to make a decision without others' opinions or acceptance. As a result, you have fewer opportunities to develop the necessary skills to handle those challenging situations that you must face throughout your life.

Self-Esteem Starts with Self-Discovery and the Recognition of Your Strengths

Acknowledging your strengths helps to improve your self-esteem. Once you identify those strengths, it will be easier to find out what your passion in life is, to make better decisions, to start having more control over your life, to express feelings that you have been keeping inside for a long time, to feel proud of what you do, and to become a self-sufficient human being. When you have low self-esteem, you risk becoming a dependent and vulnerable person.

Most aspects of our behavior are a combination of biological (nature) and environmental (nurture) factors. However, it is important that you start analyzing how people who played an important role in your life, with their actions or negative expectations (which probably were not conscious or intentional) influenced the way you feel today. Regardless of our level of education or socioeconomic status, race, ethnicity, religion, or gender, past experiences (especially those of our childhood) have a great effect in the development of our self-esteem.

When an adult's dignity was shattered during her childhood, and she was never able to break free from the information imposed by traditional teaching habits, she might have a hard time developing an adequate level of self-esteem. Others' nonconstructive criticism may lead to negative self-criticism.

One of the consequences of traditional teaching habits is that parents often set fixed conditions for their love and approval of their children, such as children having to be like them or always having to satisfy the high expectations set for them. These children may turn into adults who frequently experience irrational fears and doubts. These feelings may lead to anxiety when they face difficult or unexpected situations. It is important that when parents design a structure and formulate rules for their children, they leave some room for flexibility or negotiation. This will provide them a strong foundation for emotional growth, learning, and independence in adult life.

When adults expect the best from their children, they must offer them support and what they need most: unconditional love. As a result, in their adult lives, children will establish goals for themselves, with no fears, and be persistent and willing to take risks to achieve them, develop a healthy relationship with themselves and others, and attain self-love.

Suggestions for Improving Your Self-Esteem

The good news is that just as we learn certain behaviors that sometimes lead to a negative self-image, we can erase those behaviors from our memory, and we can learn new behaviors that will improve our self-esteem. Do you remember the chapter where I pointed out how you can turn irrational thoughts into rational ones? Rational self-talk is the best strategy to overcome low self-esteem. You can use affirmations to show yourself that you are capable of transforming your life and changing or modifying the way you think.

- Start by believing in yourself and feeling that whatever you think, do, or say is worthy. Instead of saying, "I am a fool and nobody will listen to me," you must say, "I know that my comments will help others; I will share my ideas with them." Do not think, "My past will always guide my present; I will never be able to improve my life." Instead, think, "I am ready for a new life with a wide range of perspectives; I will never be the person that I was before."

- Find a good role model you want to imitate, someone who inspires you. Observe that person's characteristics.
- Be proactive; do not wait for things to just happen without your intervention. Work hard for what you want to achieve.
- Establish realistic and very specific goals and objectives. This will make it easier to evaluate your progress.
- Avoid negative people. Develop a good support network, people who will encourage you and help you identify and celebrate your strengths.

How to Identify Your Strengths

Even though your strengths play an important role in surviving catastrophic events (which are very difficult to avoid in this world we live in), often you do not realize that you have them, so you may ignore how much they have been helping you during difficult times in your life. It is not easy to define the word *strength*. We can say that it is something that you do well all the time, although perhaps you are not aware of it. It happens so naturally that you have no awareness of how important it is.

* * * * *

Exercise 1: Finding Your Positive Attributes

The following warm-up exercise will help you embark on the difficult task of identifying your strengths. Ask yourself the following:

- Are you able to adapt to unusual or difficult situations? If yes, you are *flexible.*
- Are there times when you come up with innovative solutions for certain problems at home or in the workplace? If yes, you are *creative.*
- Do you often get across your ideas in a way that is easy for others to understand? If yes, you are a *good communicator.*
- When a friend has a problem, are you able to put yourself in his position? If yes, you can experience and understand others' emotions or feelings. You are *empathic.*
- Do you have intellectual curiosity? Do you enjoy examining things you are not familiar with? If yes, you are *open to new learning.*
- When someone says that you are lucky, do you thing that it depends on you more than on luck? Do you think this happens because you try to finish whatever you start and make an effort to do the best you can? If yes, you believe in *individual responsibility.*

Make a list of your positive attributes (please add any attributes not included above), and discuss how you will use them in the search of your true identity.

Exercise 2: Using an Autobiography to Identify Your Strengths

- An autobiography is an excellent tool to obtain insight into your life from your own perspective.
- You can write about your life history, or you can share it with others. Sharing your story with others can shed light or offer further details into how you handled difficult moments in your life.
- An autobiography can help you better understand what your life experiences meant to you. You might discover inner strengths that you are not aware of.
- An autobiography provides an excellent learning experience to reflect on how your past life experiences shaped the person you became.

The focus of this exercise is to identify your strengths considering significant events that took place in your life. Respond to the following questions:

- What has been the most difficult moment of your life?

- Identify your feelings at the time.

- How did you cope with the situation?

- What was the outcome?

- What qualities did you use to cope with this challenge?

Now that you have completed the exercise, it will be easier to understand that making connections between past and present is essential for personal growth.

- Why do you think this is true?

- What do you think are the benefits to better understand these connections?

Exercise 3: Self-Esteem Analysis

- What is your definition of *self-esteem*?

- What beliefs from your traditional teaching habits negatively affected your self-esteem? How did they develop?

- How are you planning to eliminate these beliefs in order to become a more rational and optimistic person?

- What would you suggest to people who want to develop or maintain a healthy level of self-esteem?

Exercise 4

Now, considering what you have learned and the exercises in this chapter make a final list of your strengths and celebrate them.

CHAPTER 6

What Is Spirituality?

He who has a why to live can bear almost any how.[1]
—Friedrich Nietzsche, German philosopher

Medical professionals have recognized the importance of spirituality in the healing process of the human body. Although some people relate it to religion, others associate it with works of art, enjoying nature, listening to music, or with any aspect of life that enriches the human experience. You can also get in touch with your spirituality reflecting on your experiences; practicing breathing, relaxation, and visualization exercises; and meditating, walking, or reading inspirational articles or books. It is not possible to recommend the best spiritual practice. You must look for the one that brings you peace and encourages you to meet your spiritual self.

There is not a universal consensus about the meaning of spirituality. We all have different versions of it. In my opinion, spirituality is the acknowledgment of the existence of a higher power or energy, which provides hope, strength, and support, especially during difficult times. Research suggests that people who find spirituality are better able to cope with stressful events. In general, spirituality is a way of life that offers inner peace and a sense of purpose. This transformation process could be an opportunity for your spiritual awakening.

I believe that your efforts in searching for your true identity will not be worthwhile unless you try to connect with your spiritual self. Seeking who you really are goes beyond analyzing past experiences, thoughts, and behavior, and developing self-awareness. If you have decided to transform your life, it is time to think what brings meaning and purpose to it.

As you have seen, self-change is not easy, and it has multiple dimensions. It requires a transformation of your inner thoughts and emotions and the peaceful acceptance of unpleasant past experiences. Finding spirituality could be a great resource to cope with your feelings during this process. In addition, spirituality might help you experience positive emotions about the simplest aspects of your new life.

Spirituality leads to a clearer understanding of how everything in life happens for a reason; that we can learn from what we often perceive as a negative experience. Spirituality facilitates the acceptance—without resentment or bitterness—of the challenges you must face in life, regardless of what the final outcome is.

During difficult times, sometimes your sense of spirituality is all you have. One of the benefits of finding your spiritual self is that it facilitates the acceptance of what you cannot change. Research studies show that prayer, yoga exercises, mantra repetition, and some relaxation techniques help to achieve tranquility, which generally leads to positive physiological change. We are used to "quick-fix" interventions that stem from strategies designed to stop pain. You must understand that long-lasting solutions are not outside but within you.

When you develop your spirituality, you become a more optimistic person. Spirituality helps to recognize that painful moments are inevitable; they are simply part of life. External events can produce pain; however, you often create your own suffering by not accepting life's hardships. In other words, suffering is a product of your thoughts. If someone hurt you in the past, that was surely a painful experience. Nonetheless, if you continue thinking and talking about it, and cannot forgive or free yourself from the negative emotions associated with the experience, you are allowing your past to be in control of your present. This is how you create your own suffering.

It is difficult to talk about spirituality without introducing logotherapy, a Viennese school of psychotherapy developed by the psychiatrist and neurologist Viktor Frankl, who was committed to Nazi concentration camps between 1942 and 1945. The way in which he was able to survive this experience was extraordinary. In his book *Man's Search for Meaning,*[2] Dr. Frankl said that he believes in the "defiant power of human spirit." He was capable of seeing in a very difficult and painful situation an opportunity for finding meaning in life. According to him, the spirit is capable of surviving the most negative effects of any life situation.

This theory encourages us to avoid passivity and take action, instead of feeling powerless, during difficult moments. Logotherapy impels us to do something positive with our negative experiences. It focuses on the purpose of human existence and on our search for such a meaning, regardless of life's circumstances. Based on this concept, we must commit to discover the positive aspects of adversities and the true meaning of our existence.

According to logotherapy, we do not formulate the meaning of our existence; however, we can discover it by becoming creative and developing a positive attitude toward a painful situation. Although it is not necessary to suffer to find meaning in life, this theory suggests that suffering without meaning may lead to hopelessness. Suffering is often the only thing that moves us to examine our lives in the search for meaning, which at the end may be a great source of satisfaction.

Some people seem to find satisfaction in life only through material things such as money or fame. Others seek instant or immediate gratification to escape life's worries or unsatisfactory situations. They have an urge to turn to compulsive behaviors such as excessive eating, drinking, or spending. These behaviors often reflect the need to avoid facing up to problems or negative thoughts. People who do this might end up losing control of their lives and slowing their personal growth. In the long run, the situation is not resolved; it can even get worse. They often end up empty and frustrated.

Living with a purpose encourages you to respond to negative thoughts without engaging in unhealthy behaviors. You have identified your values, your strengths, and your passion. It is now time to ask yourself, What is my purpose in life? Quiet your mind and allow your spiritual self to emerge.

The following exercise will encourage you to reflect on your purpose in life. It can be difficult, but enriching. It might require a great deal of mental effort, but it will lead to a more peaceful, interesting, and rewarding life. You will live each day to the fullest.

* * * * * *

Exercise 1: How to Find Purpose and Peace in Your Life

Respond to the following questions:

• What sense of mission do you have in your life? What do you think your unique calling in life is?

• Are you satisfied with your life? Would you prefer to be doing something different with it?

• What are those things that you enjoy doing so much that you lose perception of time?

- What do you want to offer others?

- What gives you inner peace? Do you usually set aside time to do these things?

- What keeps you going during difficult times?

- How would you like your friends to remember you?

Answering these questions will not only contribute toward your spiritual growth, but it will help you to overcome the obstacles that you will likely face along your journey to continue to learn who you really are and why you are in this world.

CHAPTER 7

How to Formulate a Personal Transformation Plan

The act of discovering who we are will force us to accept
that we can go further than we think.[1]
—Paulo Coelho, Brazilian novelist

Now that you are ready to redesign your life, you must formulate a "Personal Transformation Plan." When we realize that other people have shaped our personality without our participation, formulating an action plan becomes invigorating. Finally we feel confident that a transformation of our perspectives, beliefs, and attitudes is approaching as we work on our plan.

As I mentioned earlier, to do this you must engage in a process of self-examination and self-reflection. It is important not to lose focus on how the people in your life and your cultural values contributed to shape who you are today. While working on the plan, think about the end result. Once you find your true identity and start living by your values, you will experience a sense of freedom. An example of this feeling is what a participant in one of my groups affirmed: "I have declared war against anyone or anything that could interfere with my growth and my quest for personal freedom."

Suggestions to Formulate a Personal Transformation Plan

Think about the person you want to be and write your goals

Again, I invite you to think about what *you* really want, not about what might sound right to others. Now start writing your goals; take all aspects of your life into consideration. In this case, a goal is defined as something that you want to achieve in the long run. Later on, I will discuss the steps or objectives that will help you achieve your goals. Your goals may include the following aspects of your life, although you can add all those that you consider important:

- family
- health and wellness
- social and interpersonal life
- spiritual life
- financial management
- vocational and work life

Set simple, realistic goals that are attainable. Avoid false expectations that could become a source of stress and anxiety. Every time that you write a goal, visualize yourself enjoying your success once you have reached it.

Write your objectives or steps that you must take to accomplish your goals

You have formulated your goals and have envisioned your ideal self. Now you must think about the steps that you must take to achieve your goals. We generally call these steps "objectives," and they are short-term in contrast to the goals. These objectives or steps make it easier to achieve what you want since they often include simple things that you might already be doing in your daily life. They should be very specific; this will facilitate the evaluation and analysis of your progress.

Write down those things that you must start doing, or those that you have been doing and you think are contributing to the achievement of your goals. For example, if your goal is to learn to say no, your objective or first step may be, when someone asks you for something, to say, "I will get back to you, I need time to think about it." If you want to learn how to express your honest feelings, you can start by using a notebook to write down how you really feel. Try to set time frames for your objectives. This way you will have no choice but to evaluate your progress within the time frame you have established.

Use positive language

Use positive statements to express your goals and objectives. Remember that you are what you think. The words you choose have a powerful effect on your motivation to attain what you want. For example instead of saying, "I do not want others to abuse me," it is better to say, "I want to be valued and respected by others." These positive statements will guide your daily life.

Make a list of the challenges or obstacles that you might have to overcome during the search for the new you

Write down the internal or external obstacles that might interfere with the implementation of your transformation plan. These obstacles may include fears of failing, thinking that you must be perfect, lack of motivation, poor time management, or procrastination (postponing what you need to do). These obstacles also include people who get in your way instead of supporting you.

Think about what you will do to overcome the obstacles

Do not let obstacles make you go numb with fear. Think about possible solutions; make a plan to overcome them. Think how you are going to rely on your strengths to overcome these obstacles. Make a list of the resources that you need. Do you perhaps need to get the support of a friend or relative or the advice of a coach or therapist? You are the only one who can decide what you must have to move forward.

Try to surround yourself with people who are supportive

You must be careful when selecting who you want to share your plan with. Negativity is sometimes contagious. Avoid negative people who constantly remind you that you will not be able to achieve your goals. Share your goals and objectives with people who support you; give them permission to "keep an eye on you" once in a while. This will offer the motivation you need to remain disciplined in the pursuit of your goals.

Put your plan into action

Do not be afraid to put your plan into action. This may include modifying or altering your plan. Your plan is not carved into stone; you have the right to make changes. No one is able to transform old habits and attitudes overnight.

Evaluate your progress

Review your progress at least once weekly. Be observant and analyze your lack of progress, if this is the case. Be patient; do not be hard on yourself. If you fail, do not be discouraged. Try again and eliminate the word *frustration* from your vocabulary. If you need to rewrite your plan and make changes, remember that there is nothing wrong with this.

Celebrate your achievements

Reward yourself every time you make progress. Look at yourself in the mirror; give yourself a big hug. Do something that you enjoy to celebrate your success.

Keep learning and do not stop being self-reflective

Regardless of your age, keep learning throughout your life. Self-exploration is an ongoing process. When you do not have a response, ask yourself questions or discuss your doubts with people who share your desire to learn and to use their life experiences in their future actions. Never forget that through self-reflection, you can identify and challenge irrational assumptions acquired in the past. When you develop self-awareness, you are able to ask yourself why you are not living the life you want, and you can start doing something about it. Reflection is essential to self-improvement and personal growth.

My Personal Transformation Plan

- Write your goals. Remember that a goal is something you want to achieve in the long run. Try not to choose more than three goals.

- Write your objectives (try including estimated time frames for each objective). Remember that objectives are the steps you must take to achieve your long-term goals. Objectives are short-term.

- Write the obstacles that may keep you from achieving your goals and how you are going to overcome them.

- Make a list of people who can offer you support.

- Formulate an evaluation plan to measure your progress at least weekly. Make the necessary modifications if needed.

- Make a plan to reward yourself every time you make progress. Think of things you really enjoy.

Epilogue

Personal transformation can and does have global effects. As we go, so goes the world, for the world is us. The revolution that will save the world is ultimately a personal one.[1]
—Marianne Williamson, American author

Embarking on a journey of critical self-reflection is not an easy task, but we need to tap deeper into our minds to get to know and understand ourselves better. During our youth, we often want to change the world; however, we do not realize how important it is to change ourselves first.

On many occasions we join organizations, community groups, and committees, looking for ways to influence the course of events in society. When our attempts are met with failure, it may not occur to us that what the world needs is a change in the way we individually think and behave.

I hope that this process of self-discovery provides alternative ways to understand your life experiences and enhances your ability to engage in a process of mutual discovery and understanding with others. One of the benefits of self-knowledge and of making sense of why we think and behave the way we do is the development of empathy, which is the ability to see the world from the perspective of others. This is the key to personal and social transformation.

I hope that after you find your true identity, you can enjoy the freedom that, consciously or unconsciously, you have always been looking for. This is the first step, not just toward personal change, but toward an attitude of mutual respect that may change the world as a whole.

Notes

Introduction

[1]   Socrates, BrainyQuote.com, Xplore Inc., http://www.brainyquote.com/quotes/quotes/s/socrates101168.html. Accessed February 3, 2015.

[2]   Epictetus, BrainyQuote.com, Xplore Inc., http://www.brainyquote.com/quotes/quotes/e/epictetus149131.html. Accessed February 3, 2015.

Chapter 1

[1]   Plutarch, BrainyQuote.com, Xplore Inc., http://www.brainyquote.com/quotes/quotes/p/plutarch 161334.html. Accessed February 3, 2015.

Chapter 2

[1]   William Shakespeare, BrainyQuote.com, Xplore Inc., http://www.brainyquote.com/quotes/quotes/w/williamsha 109527.html. Accessed February 3, 2015.

[2.]   Judith S. Beck, *Cognitive Behavior Therapy: Basics and Beyond*, 2nd ed. (New York: The Guildford Press, 2011).

[3]   Albert Ellis and Debbie Joffe Ellis, *Rational Emotive Behavior Therapy* (Washington, DC: American Psychological Association, 2011).

[4]   Albert Ellis, BrainyQuote.com, Xplore Inc., http://www.brainyquote.com/quotes/authors/a/albertelli318458.html. Accessed February 4, 2015.

Chapter 3

[1] Buddha, BrainyQuote.com, Xplore Inc., http://www.brainyquote.com/quotes/quotes/b/buddha/104025.html. Accessed February 3, 2015.

[2] Daniel Goleman, *Emotional Intelligence: Why It Can Matter More Than IQ* (New York: Bantam Books, 2005).

Chapter 4

[1] Benjamin Franklin, BrainyQuote.com, Xplore Inc., http://www.brainyquote.com/quotes/quotes/b/benjaminfr378118.html. Accessed February 4, 2015.

Chapter 5

[1] Eleanor Roosevelt, BrainyQuote.com, Xplore Inc., http://www.brainyquote.com/quotes/quotes/e/eleanorroo161321.html. Accessed February 3, 2015.

Chapter 6

[1] Friedrich Nietzsche, BrainyQuote.com, Xplore Inc., http://www.brainyquote.com/quotes/quotes/f/friedrichn103819.html. Accessed February 3, 2015.

[2] Victor E. Frankl, *Man's Search for Meaning* (Boston: Beacon Press, 2006).

Chapter 7

[1] Paulo Coehlo, Twitter, https://twitter.com/paulocoelho/status/40640422358129868. Posted November 29, 2013.

Epilogue

[1] Marianne Williamson, BrainyQuote.com, Xplore Inc., http://www.brainyquote.com/quotes/quotes/m/mariannewi401955.html. Accessed February 3, 2015.

Printed in the United States
By Bookmasters